CW01674887

Walk Through a Rainbow

Ellie Collins

Illustrated by Marc Renshaw

First published in Great Britain 2020

ISBN 978-1-5272-6142-6

Ridgewell and Ducklop

Walking along in the rain one day, Washed out, dripping, dull and grey. Hood up, head down, Soaking Wet, no sign of it stopping yet.

Thunder, lightening, thick black cloud, flashing booming, crashing loud! Run for cover, seek out shelter! Slipping Sliding, helter-skelter!

Under a tree I watch the sky, the rain slows down and it starts to dry. I shake myself and stamp my feet in all the puddles down the street.

At last the sun appears, hooray! It's turning into a lovely day. Feel the heat upon your face, the rainstorm's gone to another place!

Look, look now, over your shoulder! On the horizon the colours are bolder. On the hill, across the sky a radiant ribbon catches my eye.

Red and orange, yellow and green - the most beautiful thing I've ever seen. Blue and indigo, violet too, traced in an arc of every hue.

The rain's passed by and the sun's come out
So rays of light can bounce about.

I remember a story I heard from a friend...
If you follow a rainbow right to its end...

There you find... or so I'm told... a great big pot of shining gold!
I'll follow that rainbow as far as it goes. I'll follow the colours, I'll follow my nose.

Join me under the beaming arch
We'll find the end and off we'll march

Here we go, the trail is streaming
A rosy flush is brightly gleaming

Hot and intense, a vibrant RED
It leads us in and straight ahead...

Fields of poppies and sweet scented roses
Postboxes, ladybirds, frostbitten noses

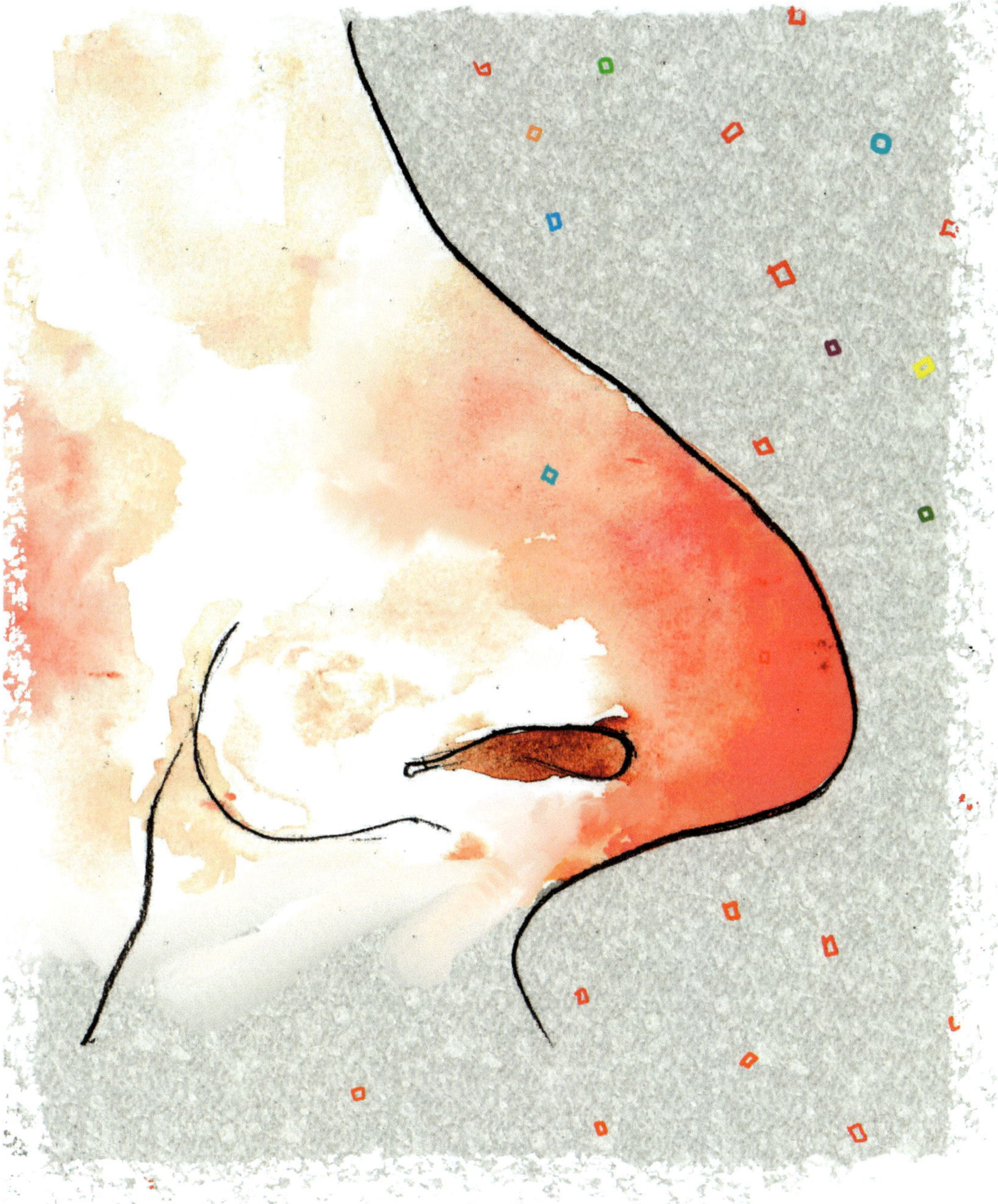

Rubies and lipstick and warm rosy cheeks. Tongues
Stained with beetroot and spilt ketchup streaks

Tomatoes and strawberries, juicy and pippy
Triangular signs warning roads might be slippy

Traffic lights change so you come to a STOP!
The glow of a fire says 'careful, it's HOT!'

Moving on, it's time to go. Which tint of the rainbow is all-aglow?

Sensational ORANGE, exciting and fun
We leap along, we bounce, we run!

Armbands and lifebuoys for swimming and sailing
Windsocks are flapping and road cones curtailing

Ginger and turmeric, spices for warming
Amber and sunrises gradually forming

Garlands of marigolds draped at a Wedding
Marmalade, sticky and perfect for spreading

Corals and Clownfish in tropical seas
Autumn leaves rustling, falling from trees

Onward now, away we skip. What colour is next on the rainbow strip?

Bathed in warmth, cheerful and mellow
We trip through a vista of dazzling YELLOW

Cheese cubes and pineapple chunks on a stick
Hot buttered sweetcorn and lollies to lick

Bananas in custard are served in a bowl
While bonbons and gummies are gobbled up whole

Bright bobbing ducks make our bathtime more fun
Tart, tangy lemons are sour on the tongue

Bumblebees buzzing, a chirping canary
The glittering tip on the wand of a fairy

Joyful, happy, off we dance. Which
rainbow hue will meet our glance?

Crisp and fresh as a homegrown bean
We stroll through restful, soothing GREEN

Freshly mown grass that is raked into piles
Toothy and Knobbly old Crocodiles

Granny Smith apples for crumbles and pies
Kermit the Frog and a pussycat's eyes

Desert-grown cacti with prickles and spines
Rainforest jungles of creepers and vines

Cool crunchy salads and hot mushy peas
Please use your tissue whenever you sneeze!

Refreshed and cool, it's time to leave.
Which bright new shade is up your sleeve?

We peacefully tiptoe through soft, dreamy BLUE
We're calm and serene as we take in the view

Whales in an ocean of icebergs and cold
Cornflowers, Sapphires, Skies to behold

Peacocks and butterflies, Soaps and Shampoos
Twinkling Starlight, a bump and a bruise

Small speckled eggs in a song thrush's nest
Ink on a letter that's sealed and addressed

Splashing around in the pool or the sea
Old denim jeans with a hole in the knee

Relaxed and rested, lets move on
Are there any more aspects to happen upon?

We sleepwalk near midnight past INDIGO Seas
We daydream through VIOLET swept by the breeze

Damsons and dangling bunches of grapes
Amethysts, aubergines, soft velvet drapes

Lilac and lavender, bristly thistles
Bubblegum popping and cheap plastic whistles

Jam smudged on tablecloths, blackcurrant spills
Sweet peas in vases on white windowsills

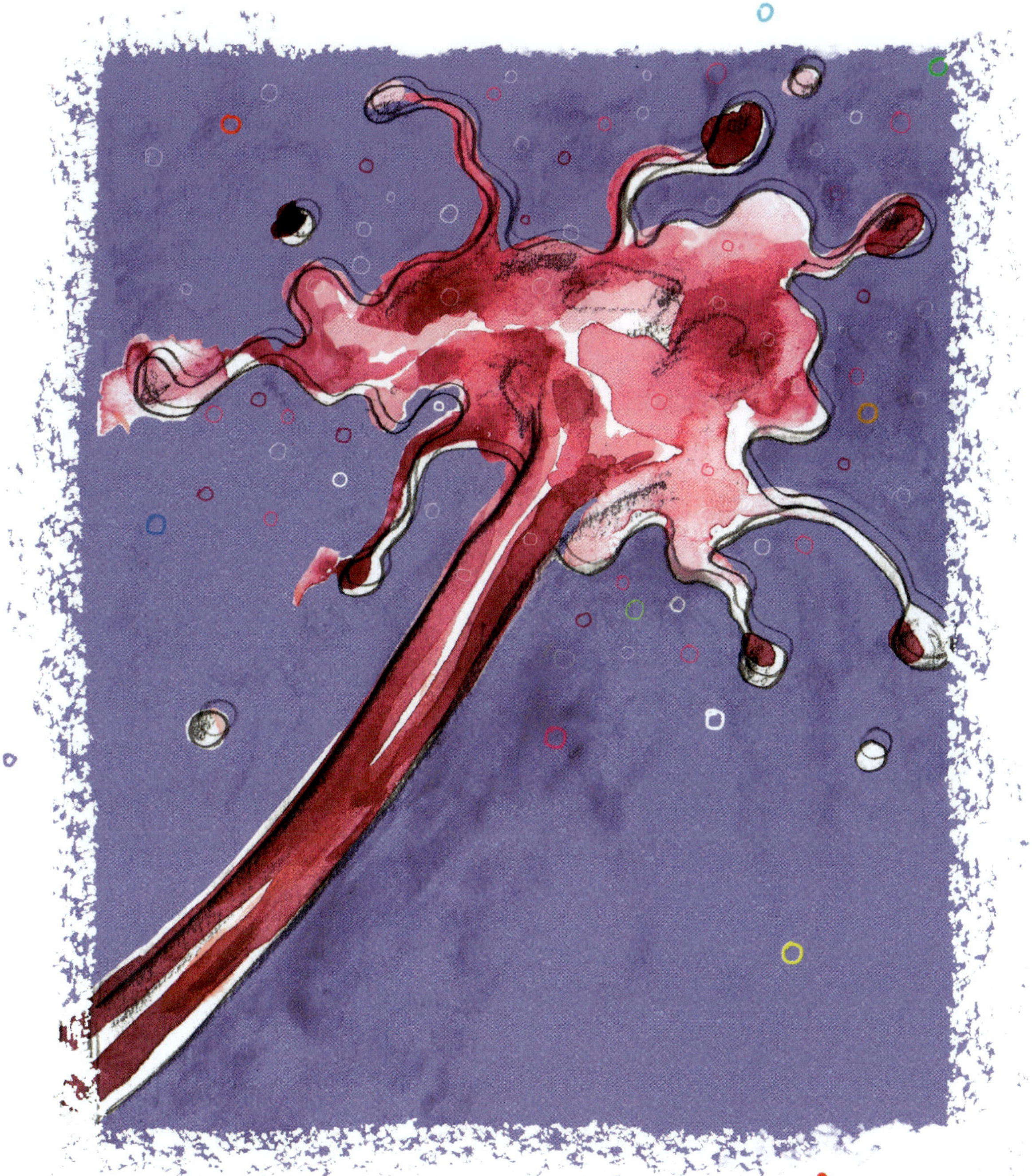

Heather that clings to a steep windswept hill
Twenty pound notes and a five dollar bill

With another step forward we're blinking our eyes
They open up fully in sudden surprise...

For the rainbow has vanished, the spectacle finished
Apart from some fluffy clouds all is diminished

Our Walk through the Spectrum has come to an end
And revealed not a solitary penny to spend...

But our colourful story can now be retold
And it's richer by far than a potful of gold!

Printed in Great Britain
by Amazon

67297101R00015